S0-AYR-245

Honesty the Best Policy

And Other Stories

By M.E. Ropes

The Religious Tract Society

Published by The Young Advent Pilgrim's Bookshelf
Marshall, North Carolina

Library of Congress Catalog Card Number: 96-97152
ISBN 1-57502-321-0

Additional copies may be obtained by sending a check (payable to Elizabeth A. Collins) for $7.30 (includes postage) to the address below. For your convenience, an order form can be found at the back of this book. To receive more information on Y.A.P.'s other materials, send a postcard with your name and address.

The Young Advent Pilgrims' Bookshelf
Elizabeth A. Collins
649 Paw Paw Rd.
Marshall, NC 28753

Printed in the USA by

MORRIS
PUBLISHING

3212 E. Hwy 30
Kearney, NE 68847
800-650-7888

CONTENTS

Honesty the Best Policy;

or, Molly's Special Providence

"WANTED — A man and his wife (without encumbrances) to take charge of a house for three months during the absence of the family, and to superintend spring cleaning. The highest references indispensable."

"How would that do, Molly?"

"Nicely, so far as we are concerned, but we don't know how we should suit the folks. Then as to the references, Sam; of course we can't expect to get a situation without good testimonials. Why, think of poor Fred Wylde, how long he has been out of place, just because he was turned away for theft, and without a character."

"For *supposed* theft, Molly, 'twasn't ever proved. But there will be no difficulty about our characters, dear. Our clergyman, Mr. Parsons, and my old master, and your mistress, would each give us character, or a letter of recommendation. Why, Molly, you know they would have secured me a good place long ago, if I hadn't been too weak to work hard, after that long illness of mine. But this would suit if we can get it, and it would be something to be earning a trifle, and not to be paying rent."

That same evening, taking with him the needful papers, Sam Preston went to the address indicated in the advertisement, saw the master of the house, and was fortunate enough to secure the situation.

We pass over all the preliminaries, suffice it to say, that the Prestons stored their small stock of cottage furniture in a neighboring tradesman's lumber room, and moved into Linton Lodge the same day that the family of Mr. Markham left it, establishing themselves as comfortably as circumstances would permit by night.

"The master said," remarked Sam that evening as they sat at tea, "that any rubbish we find about the house, odds and ends left in holes and corners, we might keep."

"There isn't much that would be of use to us, Sam," replied Molly, laughing. "Unless, indeed, it were waste paper, which, perhaps, we could send to the mills. There's a quantity of that; indeed, there's a room upstairs that seems just full of it. Old newspapers, and wrappers, and books of advertisements, and no end of circulars. We can look through them some day, and make up a sack or two, since Mr. Markham gives us leave."

In a few days the Prestons had become accustomed to their temporary home. The kitchen and a bedroom downstairs had not been left in the dismantled condition of the rest of the house, but were quite comfortably furnished with all that was necessary.

Linton Lodge, too, was situated not so far from the Prestons' former house but that Molly could still take in needlework for her old customers, and carry it home when finished, without the expense of a railway journey.

Of course Sam and Molly could never leave the house at the same time, so that they were unable to go to church together, but this was the only thing that they at all minded.

Molly had a good deal of work in hand just now, and Sam was very busy doing odds and ends of carpentering and repairing about the house and out-buildings, and in working in the garden, which had been greatly neglected of late, owing to the illness of the gardener. So it was quite two weeks or more before they found time to look over and sort the heaps of paper in the lumber room — heaps of which were apparently the accumulation of years, saved probably always in the hope that they would come in usefully some day.

Molly began with the work bright and early one morning, while Sam was cleaning his own boots and hers downstairs.

Suddenly he heard an exclamation, or rather a cry of surprise, from his wife, and in a moment more she came running down with a flushed face and sparkling eyes, and

DICOVERY OF THE NOTES

a paper in her hand, while in her apron she held some more folded sheets.

"Oh, Sam, what do you think?" and the little woman held up a ten-pound note before her husband's astonished eyes. "Fancy, dear, I found it among these folded circulars. I was undoing them all, so as to be sure to sort the paper properly, and this dropped out of one of them. Oh, I'm so glad, Sam, aren't you? Now you can go down to the sea-side for a week, and get quite strong and like your old self, and — and — *perhaps* I could have a new dress; mine is so shabby for Sunday wear; and — "

"Stop a bit, Molly, my child, what are you talking about?" exclaimed Sam. "That money isn't ours, you know."

"Not ours? Why, Sam? The folks gave us the rubbish — all of it — and if we've found this among the rubbish, why, it's ours of course. It seems to me plain enough."

"Just think a minute, Molly dear. Do you suppose that Mr. Markham when he told us we might do what we liked with the rubbish, knew that there was a ten-pound note in the waste paper? Now be your own honest self, little woman, and answer my question truly."

Molly glanced down at the tempting bit of paper in her hand, realising to the full all that she and Sam should forfeit in giving it up. But with her husband's honest eyes looking full into her face, and her husband's faith in her warm at her heart, she said — somewhat reluctantly, it must be confessed — "Well, no, Sam, of course I couldn't think that Mr. Markham knew of this note."

"Good; then of course, too, it need hardly be said that not knowing, he did not intend us to have it; eh, Molly?"

"Yes," murmured Molly.

"Then," pursued Sam, "if we took what we were not intended to have, and therefore what we had no real right to, we should just be thieves — nothing more nor less."

"Oh, Sam, not thieves!"

"Yes, dear, just that. There's nothing for it, Molly, but to write a letter to Mr. Markham saying that we've found the note, and giving number. Then, whatever he says about it, we shall abide by."

"Well, I suppose you're right, Sam," said Molly; "indeed you most always are. But I can't help being disappointed, for when I found the note, I said to myself,

'That's a Special Providence;' and it seemed as if God had sent it to help us afterwards, when our stay here was over, and we should be looking out for a new home."

"Well, wifie, and I shouldn't wonder if it turned out a Special Providence after all," replied Sam, smiling. "Providence does not always work just as we expect, but it may be none the less special for that. Of one thing we may be sure," he added, speaking more solemnly; "that if we act up to our sense of right, and to the conscience that God has given us — without reckoning either what we have to give up, or what may come of our actions, God will overrule all for the best, and make things work together for good."

That very day Sam wrote a letter mentioning the finding of the note and the number of it. And when the packet was despatched, Molly began to feel more settled in her own mind, and surer than ever that her husband had taken the only right course.

Nor did the young wife have cause to regret, on any account, that Sam had been so firm about the money she had found.

A few days later came a most kind note from Mr. Markham, commending in cordial terms the conduct of the Prestons, expressing his pleasure at finding them such trustworthy, honorable people.

"But," he added, "you have unconsciously done a good turn to some one whom probably you do not at all know; for you gave me the chance to make reparation for the suspicion and dismissal of a servant who, it now appears, was not guilty of the fault with which I charged him. Nine months ago, I engaged a butler, but before he had been with me long, I one day missed a ten-pound note, which I knew I had left on my library writing-table, when I was suddenly called out of the room. Quite unexpectedly, I was absent from the library for some hours on that occasion, but when I returned the note was gone.

"No one had been into the room, it was proved, but the butler and the housemaid, and the latter was an old servant who had lived with us for twenty years, and who was above suspicion. So I dismissed the butler, though he protested his innocence. Fortunately I had the number of the note, and it corresponds exactly with that you gave me: and I can now only imagine that the wind blowing in at the library window that day, had perhaps blown the bank-note into the rubbish basket lying below, and that it had slipped into one of the circulars, of which I had put a quantity into the basket pretty nearly every morning. The basket must have been emptied in the usual way into the lumber room, my housemaid having an old-fashioned prejudice against burning papers found in the rooms until they have been looked through.

"I shall now write to my former butler, telling him that I shall shortly be again in want of a servant, and that I should be glad to take him back, if he is willing to come.

"Now I think of it, he came from your part of the town; it is just possible you may know him. His name is Frederick Wylde."

At this Molly, who had been looking over Sam's shoulder, jumped up and clapped her hands.

"Frederick Wylde!" she cried, "poor

Fred, my own cousin's husband! And he would never tell us the name of the people who had sent him away. Why, Sam, I can see his face now, and his poor wife's too, when he said to me, 'Cousin Molly, this is too great a trial for me to speak of to most people, and I would rather not tell even *you*, who my master was. But I hope and earnestly pray that the Lord may make it plain some day that I didn't rob those whose bread I was eating.'"

"And the Lord *has*, you see, Molly dear," replied Sam, with joyful earnestness.

There was a moment's silence, during which Molly looked very grave. Then she said very humbly and sweetly, "Sam, if you hadn't been wiser and better than I, poor Fred would never have been cleared, and think how dreadful that would have been!"

"And what about your Special Providence, Molly?"

"Why, this *is* a Special Providence if ever there was one," replied Molly, emphatically.

In the course of the next week the Prestons had a call one day from Frederick Wylde, who came to tell them of a letter he had received from Mr. Markham, containing the good news that his innocence was proved. His thankfulness and delight were so great that Sam and Molly were quite touched, and when Fred described how, when the good news came, he had said to his wife, "Well, Jenny, this *is* a Special Providence! An answer to our prayer has come in quite an unexpected way" — Molly first glanced at her husband, then coloured to the roots of her pretty hair, and ended by bursting into tears, thereby much astonishing poor Fred, until she explained the great temptation that had assailed her, and which she had called a Special Providence — and expressed her thankfulness that she had not been allowed to follow her own wishes.

The house-cleaning occupied the last four weeks of the Prestons' sojourn at Linton Lodge; but all was completed in good time; and just two days before the rest of the family arrived, Mr. Markham came up from the country to town to give some orders, and see to a few arrangements in the house.

After sundry questions about things in general, he suddenly said,

"Tell me, Preston, have you a situation in prospect when you leave here?"

"No, sir, I'm sorry to say not."

"Would you have any objection to one at the sea-side?"

"Oh dear no, sir; that's of all the things what I should like best," replied Sam; "the doctor told me that sea air was what I needed."

"Because," continued Mr. Markham, "I have a house down at Fairtide, in Blankshire, and the man who took care of it is just dead, and I want some one to put in his place. It is hardly necessary to say that I require a trustworthy person, and you have proved yourself thoroughly so. Therefore I cannot do better, I think, than offer you the place. It will be a permanent situation, if we are mutually satisfied, and your work will be to keep the house and take care of the garden, and when any of my family come down, as we do occasionally for a day or two, to wait on us. Your wife can cook, I suppose?"

"Yes, sir, I'm a pretty good cook," replied Molly, smiling and blushing.

"Well, then, we shall consider that settled," said Mr. Markham; "that is, if the terms suit you. I give thirty shillings a week, your fuel found, and the use of the vegetables and fruit in the garden when none of us happen to be there. How will that do for you?"

"Thank you, sir, we could wish for nothing better," responded Sam; and so the matter ended.

"Well this is a Special Providence, and no mistake!" exclaimed Molly, when Mr. Markham had gone. "How much more good that ten-pound note has done us than if I'd spent it. First there's the clearing of poor Fred's character, and giving him back his situation, and now it has given us a good home to go to straight from here, and enough to live on, and lay by too, and the sea air for you, which was just what you needed."

"Molly dear," replied Sam, gravely but tenderly, "all God's dealings with us are Special Providences. Special, because He makes each one of His children His special care, and is always working for their good. But, my dear wife, we have at least learned one great lesson from this ten-pound note; and it is that *to do right*, no matter at what apparent sacrifice, is not only the honest,

Christian way, but the best policy in the long run. Don't you agree with me, Molly?"

And Molly, for very joy and gladness, and feeling to the full in her happy little heart the force and truth of Sam's words, threw her arms round her husband's neck, and whispered, as she kissed him, *"Indeed, Sam, I do."*

"God Bless You, Bob"

OB CASTANET was a fisherman, the finest young fellow in the sea-side village of Saylaway. Nor were his looks the best part of him, though his worst enemies (if he had any) must have acknowledged that if a well-developed, vigorous form, an intelligent face, and clear, honest blue eyes, at once tender and daring, were any advantages, Bob had some pretensions to the kind of beauty which contributes not a little to a man's popularity.

Bob's face did not belie his nature. Frank, fearless, manly, honest, and tender, — so those found him who had most to do with him; and his faults were readily forgiven by the affection he inspired. Bob had lately married, and his wife, a handsome girl from a neighbouring village, had been somewhat envied by many of the Saylaway maidens, upon whose hearts young Castanet's handsome face had made an impression.

But now four or five months of married life were over, and people were getting used to the marriage; and as for the young wife, she had become so attached to her little cliff-side home, that she would hardly believe she had been there so short a time.

Marion Castanet was one of those high-spirited, impulsive girls, whose quick temper and pride often get them into trouble, but whose warm affections and honest repentance usually prevent their going very far in a wrong course.

Marion sincerely loved and ardently admired her husband; but after the first weeks of married life had gone by, with their lover-like demonstrations and willing subjection, a little of her strong, impulsive character had begun to show itself; and as Bob, with all his virtues, was not quite an angel, an occasional dispute would arise, and would sometimes bring heart-ache and remorse in its train.

One morning Marion sat down to breakfast in no amiable mood. Bob's fishing for the last week had not been quite so successful as usual, and his wife was somewhat short of money.

She had promised herself a new autumn bonnet, with which she had wished to dazzle the eyes of less fortunate women at church on the following Sunday; and now there was no chance of getting it. Then, too, the last batch of bread had turned out heavy and sad, and Bob shook his head with an odd expression in his face of amusement and pretended disgust, as he cut off a big spongy slice of the new loaf to eat with his herring. Even the herring had got charred in the cooking, and the coffee was thick, and Marion felt as if everything had gone wrong, and her temper consequently did not improve.

"I hope these 'ere purwisions won't lie heavy on my digesture," said Bob, rather mischievously, looking up from his sad bread and charred herring with a mock-pensive air, and meeting his wife's eye in which the fire of anger was smouldering.

"'Tain't my fault if they do!" replied she, with emphasis.

"No," replied Bob, who had a sailor's love of teasing, "it's mine, I shouldn't wonder. All the world knows that the man's business is to mix the bread and cook the wittles."

"You seem to think it's a man's work to grumble and find fault," replied Marion, with some heat. "You don't know what a hard life a woman's is."

"Well, come along with me to-day, and see if you like my work any better," said Bob with a wink and a half-smile.

Now it had always been a joke against Marion that she could not be in a boat ten minutes without being sea-sick, and this remark, which at any other time would only have provoked her laughter, now made her still more angry.

"You're a heartless, cruel man!" exclaimed she, rising from the table, "and I wish I'd never married you, that I do! If you're like this after five months, what'll you be after five years? I'm sick of it all, that I am!"

"Well, if this is the way you're a-goin' to behave," replied Bob, whose temper was also somewhat roused, "we shan't neither of us die of happiness." And he, too, rose from his seat, and left the room to get ready for his boat.

His irritation, however, had subsided when he returned to the little kitchen, where his wife was standing at the dresser washing up the crockery. He laid his hand on her shoulder.

"Good-bye, my girl," said he. "I didn't mean to vex you, or to be vexed myself. Kiss me and let me go, Marion. Say, 'God bless you, Bob,' as you always do."

What perverse spirit had possession of Marion's heart just then? She moved away from her husband's caressing hand, and answered never a word.

"I hope to be back by the evening," said the young man. Then, once more stooping over her, he whispered, "Kiss me, and say, 'God bless you, Bob.' Just once, Marion, dear little wife, just once!"

But Marion turned away with a defiant toss of her head, and with her wildly beating heart full of proud obstinacy in battle with yearning love for her husband. Another moment, and she rushed upstairs to her bedroom and locked herself in.

Then she heard Bob's footsteps down below, heard him close the door of the house after him, and then she knew he had gone.

All day Marion Castanet went about her work listlessly and with an aching heart. In vain she tried to excuse herself for her temper in the morning. Her conscience reproached her bitterly, and she was very miserable. She could not eat, so she cooked no dinner for herself, but only drank a cup of tea, and then sat down to her sewing.

Towards afternoon the wind began to rise, the clouds gathered, the sea freshened.

Marion was sitting in the little kitchen, which was at the back of the house and faced the sea. With growing anxiety she watched the signs of the coming gale.

Sea-birds flew screaming hither and thither; and now, far as the eye could reach, the white crest of the angry waves leaped and tossed in growing violence. Dark and howling, the night descended upon the village of Saylaway, and heavy grew the heart of poor Marion Castanet.

WATCHING FOR BOB

Her husband might be far out to sea, and unable to get back. What might not happen to him! And oh! saddest of all – in anger she had suffered him to go without her parting kiss and blessing.

"Oh, Bob, my Bob!" she sighed, as she gazed out across the waste of water, "if harm should come to you, I should die of grief!"

The night deepened, and still the wind increased, and the sea rushed and roared.

The little cottage rocked like a house of cards in the gale, and Marion grew more and more anxious.

Again and again she stepped to the door, and stood there watching the wild dark clouds rolling up across the sky, and the snowy surf of the in-coming tide stretching round the rocky coast like a girdle.

Eleven o'clock came, but Bob had not returned, and Marion was in great fear. At a quarter past a knock came at the door, and she flew to open it. She knew it could not be her husband, for he always entered with a latch-key; but she almost shrieked with dismay and suspense when she saw that her visitor was Hal Huckerback, a fisherman living not far off.

"What is it?" eagerly asked Marion. "Tell me! It's bad news?"

"Yes, Mrs. Bob, I'm afraid it be," he replied. "There's a man just come into the village, and he says there's a boat been washed ashore lower down on the coast, and the name on her is the 'Pearl.'"

Marion gave a cry, and staggered back against the wall. The "Pearl" was her husband's boat. Her worst fears then must be confirmed. Bob, her manly, loving, tender husband, was lost — gone to his death without her kiss on his lips, or her blessing upon his head.

Hal said what he could to comfort her, but she did not hear him, so at last he shut the door and went away. Then she managed to crawl upstairs, and to throw herself on her knees by the bedside.

"Oh, what shall I do? What shall I do?" she moaned. "My heart is broke! Oh, Bob! my own Bob, that loved me so. And I wouldn't kiss him and say good-bye; and he went away and he's lost, and I didn't pray, 'God bless him!' Oh, my husband! Oh, Bob, my love, my love!"

"Marion!"

Whose voice could say that name so tenderly?

Dumb with the reaction from a terrible shock, the young wife looked up. Yes! It was Bob's own dear self that stood beside her. With a sobbing cry, a wholesome gush of tears, she threw herself into his arms.

There was silence for a few moments. Then Marion raised her head and kissed her husband, murmuring like a repentant child the words she should have said in the morning, "Good-bye! God bless you, Bob!"

After a while, the young man told his wife the story of his escape. He said that he was trying to get home, when the gale came on with great violence, and one of the seams in his boat (which was an old one, and hardly fit for much rough weather) gave way, and began to let the water in. He could not stop the leak, or bale and manage the boat at the same time, and every minute the gale was freshening, and the danger increasing. Looking round, he espied a coasting vessel not far off, and he made signs to her that he was in distress.

The men in the coaster immediately attended to his signal, and finally got him on board. The fishing-boat was plugged as well as she could be at such a time, and then was towed along astern, but the rope broke, and thus the little craft was washed ashore, and was seen by the man who had sent through Hal Huckerback the report to poor Marion.

So, after all, Bob was safe; but Marion, as long as she lived, never forgot the terrible anguish of that day; and from all we have heard of the young couple since, we may feel quite sure that they have had no more serious quarrels.

We do not mean that Marion's fault was quite cured, but that the young wife had learned a lesson which led her to struggle daily against her besetting sin, and in God's strength to seek to overcome it.

If ever she showed signs of rising temper her husband would steal to her side, and kiss her, saying softly, "Say, God bless you, Bob!" and this was a sort of understanding between them, a reminder of the past, which never failed in its effect.

Taught By Sorrow

WHERE are you taking that pair of clumpers, Sam?" said a man to a friend of his, whom he met in the street one day, and who was carrying a pair of boots much in need of repair.

"Oh! I'm going to the cobbler's round the corner of Church Street. Will Hopkins is his name, ain't it?"

"Now look ye here, Sam!" said the first speaker. "Don't you take those boots to Will Hopkins, unless you don't want them for a month or two."

"A month or two, Tom? Why, I want 'em back to-morrow."

"Then don't you give the job to him, that's all."

"What's the matter with the man's work?" asked Sam, patting the soles of the boots with his broad hands.

"Nothing on earth as I knows on," replied Tom; "only he drinks so, that half the time he is idling about. How that poor wife of his lives, I can't think; but they do say as she's got a decline of the lungs, or something as I don't rightly understand."

"Well, I may as well find another cobbler, as this one ain't steady. Good morning to you." And Sam went away down the street, and Tom returned to his work in a neighbouring garden.

Alas! it was all too true.

Will Hopkins, with his gentle, patient wife and little child, might have been a prosperous and happy man, for he was clever at his trade, and had naturally a kind disposition. But of late years he had yielded more and more to the influence of evil companions, until now he had become quite a slave to drink, and his work was neglected, his character ruined, while his wife and child were allowed to suffer sometimes from actual want.

One day he had received a little more money than usual, and when evening came he ceased working, and began to get ready to go off to the public-house, where so many of his hours were spent and such a large proportion of his earnings was wasted.

His wife stole up to him, just as he was putting on his coat.

"Will," said she, "to please me don't go out to-night. I feel very ill, and little Willie, he's fretty; and we'd be so glad — him and me — if you'd stay with us. Don't go, dear Will, and we'll all be so happy together."

Will hesitated. His wife's face, once so bright and blooming, now so haggard and white, was upturned to his, and looked paler even than usual. Her large eyes — the eyes into which he loved to gaze during the courting days — were too large now, and full of that sorrowful pleading which is twin sister to tears.

For a moment the man stood irresolute. Then, like a fascinating picture, there came before his mind's eye the brightness, the warmth, the hilarity of the fatal gin-palace, in contrast with his own poor home. His mind was made up.

"Jenny," said he, "I *must* go to-night; there's a lot of fellows I've promised to meet; but to-morrow I'll spend with you and little Bob, see if I don't!"

All that Jenny said was unavailing. She unclasped her trembling hands from her husband's arm, and he went his way.

It was very late before he reached home. Though not really drunk, he had taken enough to make him unnaturally excited; and, to his horror, as he turned the key in the lock, he was met on the threshold, not by his wife, but by a neighbour, a woman living close by.

"Is anything wrong?" he faltered, feeling that his question was a mockery.

"Yes, Mr. Hopkins, very wrong indeed. God help her, poor Jenny!"

In another moment Will was upstairs, in the room where his wife — his uncomplaining, loving wife — was lying. The doctor stood by the bedside, with his fingers on the patient's wrist.

Softly he laid the hand down, and made

a sign of silence to poor Will, who gazed horror-struck at his wife, who was breathing in quick, short, laboured gasps. Jenny opened her eyes, and smiled at her husband, but the doctor beckoned him away outside the bedroom door.

Will hardly knew what the medical man said to him. He only caught the words, "Must have been ailing a long time—no hope—acute inflammation."

We pass over that dreadful night. With the morning's dawn, that sweet mother and wife had gone to sleep, to await the resurrection day. There, in the dim morning light, the bereaved man was sitting with his head upon his hands, dumb with the knowledge of his wife's death, when a faint cry roused him. He started and turned to the little crib where the two-year old child had been sleeping. More tenderly than ever before, the father lifted the little one, and folded him in his arms.

"Oh, my poor motherless baby!" moaned the strong man, as the child wailed for his mother. And, overcome by a sense of his own grief, his helplessness, his sin before God, he sank on his knees by his dead wife's bed, and uttered words in his agony—words of prayer of which he had not thought since he was a child at Sunday school: "Father, I have sinned against heaven, and before Thee, and am no more worthy to be called Thy son. Lord, help me!"

There never yet was a hand that grasped the Almighty arm in vain. There never yet was an earnest cry for help that failed to reach the Heavenly Father's ear and heart. And in that hour of pain the great Teacher drew near to the stricken man, and the soul that had slighted other calls was now taught by sorrow.

Jenny Hopkin's funeral took place in a few days, and the lonely widower returned to his home a saddened man, but wiser and better far. This was soon discovered by the neighbours, who did all they could to comfort and cheer him. Will's good impressions and resolutions did not weaken; he began to live a new life—a life of soberness and industry, of growing nearness to his God and Saviour.

"Tell you what, Sam!" said Tom to his friend, when he next met him, "you can take

Will Hopkins as many boots to mend *now* as you please, for a more sober or industrious cobbler never used a last."

"Ay, ay," replied Sam, gravely; "but it ain't anything to laugh about. The preacher was a-saying the other night as how God breaks our heart's sometimes to mend our souls; and I tell you, Tom, Will's heart's been broke, and it's a lesson for us all. Them as nothing else won't learn, has to be learned by sorrow."

A Good Tit for a Bad Tat

LICK, CLICK, whiz and whirr — click, click, like a fairy steam-engine ever on the go. From whence does the sound come? Follow me, gentle reader, and mind how you go, for the garret is higher yet, and the way to the abode of the fairy engine is like the spider's parlour, "up a winding stair." Here we are at last and we open the door a little, and peep in. What a bare cold room! One wee window, no fire, a turn-up bedstead in the corner, with a three-legged stool beside it; and in the window — placed so that all the light there is shall fall upon it — is the fairy engine;

nothing, after all, but a matter of-fact sewing machine.

Click, Click, whiz and whirr! on go the impish wheels; in and out flies the eager needle; lower and lower over the work bends the busy toiler.

Suddenly she stops, raises her head, and straightening her back, glances at the clock on the wall. The face that uplifts itself shows a broad, calm brow, dark eyes, very tired-looking in the lids. A sweet pensive mouth, with a shadow of patient suffering in the sensitive lips. The figure appears of moderate height, but is bowed a little with the incessant stooping. There! You have before you the portrait of Esther Makepeace as she sat by her sewing-machine one afternoon in the waning wintry light.

"Finished at last!" she murmured, as she rose and stretched herself wearily. "Finished at last; and only just in time. Mrs. Lawson said she must have it before dark, and folks are so particular at the shops." So saying, she folded her work, added it to a pile of garments lying on the stool, and wrapped the whole in a piece of brown paper. To slip on a little dark bonnet, and throw an old rain-cloak over her shoulders, did not take a moment. Then, tucking the parcel under her arm, she left her room, and began to grope her way down the narrow staircase, which was quite dark by this time. All of a sudden she struck her foot against something heavy, and only just saved herself from falling, while the something bounded from step to step, scattering fragments of a hard substance right and left.

At the noise, a door opened half-way down the stairs, and a shrill, cracked voice called out: "Who's that spilling my coals? I can't leave 'em for a minute but something must go and upset 'em."

"I'm very sorry, Mrs. Twells," said Esther, gently; "but it was quite dark, and I caught my foot against the box. I didn't know it was there, or I'd have come down more careful."

"Oh! you would, would you?" replied the old woman, crossly; "which I don't believe it neither. There ain't one of you young ones as would be at the trouble of minding where you put your feet for the sake of a poor old woman like me."

"Oh, don't say so, Mrs. Twells!" said Esther; "I really am very sorry, and I'll take more care another time — indeed I will."

"I dare say," retorted Mrs. Twells; "promises being like pie-crust, it's likely you'll keep them; but there! it ain't no use wasting more words."

While the old woman was scolding away she had brought a light, and Esther, on her knees, was picking up the coals and restoring them to the box. Then she lifted the box and carried it into the old woman's room, making no reply to the unkind words which had come only too readily from the lips of her whom she was trying to serve. Nevertheless, as she finished her task and hurried on with her parcel, her lips quivered at the remembrance of the hard words which she had certainly not deserved. But Esther had long since learned from the greatest Teacher that ever lived not to return railing for railing; and now she would not even suffer her mind to dwell too long upon what had pained her, but forgave the old woman in her heart, and tried to forget the unpleasant little incident.

The needlework was delivered safely

into the hands of Mrs. Lawson, and Esther received the small sum of money which her industry had gained. Very small it was; but the girl had never been used to luxuries, and was glad to be able, however hardly, to earn her own living.

The air was cold and frosty, and Esther trudged home very quickly; she was too thinly clad to loiter on the way. "How glad I shall be to get to bed to-night!" she sighed, as she began to mount the dark stairs. "I can go directly after tea, if I like, for my work is done, and tommorow is Sunday."

Just as Esther came to that part of the staircase upon which Mrs. Twell's door opened, she thought she heard a sob. She listened a moment, and heard another. At once forgetting the old woman's unkind treatment of herself, and thinking only how to help or comfort, she knocked at the door. "Come in," said a choked voice, and Esther entered. Old Widow Twells was standing up near the table, holding a letter in her hand, and sobbing and crying bitterly.

"Have you had bad news from your son, Mrs. Twells?" asked Esther kindly; "or what's the matter?"

"WHAT HAVE I DONE BUT SPILL MY INK-BOTTLE ALL OVER IT!"

The old woman turned her wet face towards the visitor, for a moment unable to speak.

"No, no, it ain't that!" replied she; "but just look at this letter! A whole week, as you might say, and half a dozen lines at the time, I've been writing to this soldier boy, and what have I done but spill my ink-bottle all over it! And now read it he never could, nor write it again I never can."

Esther looked at the paper. Sadly blotted it was indeed, so that in some places whole lines were illegible. For one moment there was silence, then she said, "Let me write it out for you, Mrs. Twells. Some of this I can make shift to read, and what I can't you shall tell me. I can write pretty quick, and it'll be a pleasure to me to serve you."

Mrs. Twells stared at Esther with unmistakable surprise; and then she threw the paper down on the table with a passionate gesture.

"Well, you *are* a good girl!" exclaimed she; "and I'd say Yes, and thank yer, if it weren't for them coals as I made such a fuss about."

Esther smiled. "Never mind them," said she; "that's all forgotten and done with. Let me sit down at once and write this letter for you."

So Esther sat down, giving up, without a murmur, the long rest to which she had been looking forward. Patiently she wrote line after line of the old woman's letter, copying some of it, and writing other parts from dictation. It was late before the task was ended, and the girl rose to go. As she did so, Mrs. Twells rose too, and laying her wrinkled hand on her visitor's arm, she said: —

"Esther, I've been a-wondering what it is as makes you different from most people. It ain't as how you're richer nor us, nor you ha'n't got many friends; and yet, though you keeps yourself to yourself in a general way, whether it's Mrs. Jack's sick baby crying, or whether it's poor, cross old Widder Twells as spills ink on her letter, you've got a helping hand ready, and no crooked words for them as speaks crooked to you. Now I wish you'd tell me your secret what makes you like this, for if I can get it, mayhap it'll make me different."

Esther did not smile, though she might have been excused for so doing. She only looked earnestly into the old woman's face and said: "I'm not near so good as you think, Mrs. Twells; but I am trying to be and if you want my secret, which after all is no secret, why, here it is. It's just to believe that we're nothing of ourselves, and that Christ is everything; it's just to trust in Him, and to love Him, and to follow Him, and to love others for His dear sake. That is all my secret, Mrs. Twells."

What more may have passed between the two women we do not know, for just then Mrs. Twells discovered that the door was a little ajar, and rose to shut it; but perhaps we have heard enough to come to the conclusion that Esther Makepeace's retaliation was the only right kind of revenge, and that "Tit for Tat," played thus, can never be a source of unhappiness or mutual hatred.

Will's Victory

THE coastguardsman, Michael Ruffit, was well-known and respected by most persons in the seaport. He had spent his life upon the sea, and at one time was the owner of a little coasting vessel, *The Lively Polly*. He went by the name of Skipper Mike as a rule; and a kind-hearted fellow he was, and much liked by the villagers. So when sharp sickness came into the seaman's little home, and laid its heavy

hand upon Mike's wife, the neighbours
were very anxious and much disturbed;
and when God's pale angel Death followed quickly, the sympathy of Mike's
friends knew no bounds, and they vied
with each other in doing their best to comfort and help him in his bereavement. But
Mike was not the only mourner in the little
cottage, for he had a son, a boy about
twelve years old, who had dearly loved his
mother, and who missed her sorely.

Will Ruffit was a fine manly youth, but
of rather a silent, reserved disposition. His
mother had been his great friend and ad-
viser; and now that she was gone he was
lonely indeed. Will spent much of his time
on the water, and sometimes went on short
coasting voyages; when on shore, he used
to find work among the fishermen and
boatmen of the village, mending nets and
rigging, and doing odd jobs of any sort that
might fall in his way.

Will clung to his mother's memory with
a tenacity which had something quite
touching about it; and when, after two years
of loneliness and discomfort, his father
spoke of shortly bringing a new wife to the

old home at Offing, Will's indignation
knew no bounds.

"I'll never speak to her, much less love
her!" he said, fiercely, when Mike had left
the cottage one morning after informing
Will of his intentions. "How can I bear a
new mother here? I'll run away, or I'll go
and live with the neighbours, but I won't
never call her 'Mother,' nor say a civil word
to her." So saying, the boy walked out of the
house and down to the shore. He felt rest-
less and miserable, and longed to be quite
alone, so, borrowing a small row boat which
was lying idle, he pushed off and began to
pull along the coast.

As may be imagined, his thoughts were
fully occupied; indeed, so intent was he
upon the one subject which was now
engrossing his attention, that he did not
notice how time was passing, and he suddenly became conscious that he was a long
way from home, and, judging from the position of the sun, that he must have been out
several hours. He began to feel somewhat
tired, too, and very hungry; so, having a few
pence in his pocket, he thought he would
pull to shore and see if he could not

purchase some food. There was no surf, so he rowed up towards the beach, till the keel touched the sand, then, jumping overboard, he waded to shore and fastened his boat to a ring in the remains of an old breakwater. The tide was rising, and Will knew that the boat would float again in an hour's time.

The cliffs were low just here, and it only took him a few moments to mount and to knock at the door of a cottage that stood at the head of the rugged pathway up which he had come. The door was opened by a bright-looking woman. She was neatly dressed, and her rich brown hair was put back from her face in smooth braids, which formed a strong contrast to the rough style of hair-dressing common among the fishermen's wives and daughters.

"What do you please to want?" asked the woman, with a smile; and Will, his shyness overcome by the voice and manner of the speaker, said frankly, "I've rowed a long way, and I'm tired and hungry; could you give me something to eat? I can pay for what I have."

"Come in, my lad," was the reply; and thus invited Will entered. In a few minutes a good meal of broth and bread and a piece of cheese was set before the hungry boy, who did ample justice to the provision. But when he took out his little leather bag to pay for what he had eaten, his hostess said, "Nay, nay, my lad; put up your purse again; we're not so poor — father and me — that we can't give a meal to a traveller, and him a sailor, as are all our kith and kin."

So Will had to put away his money; and somehow the woman's gentle ways and kind words led him on, till, contrary to his usual habits, he found himself talking away quite easily. He sat there about an hour, then rose and, with hearty thanks to his entertainer, took his leave. He reached home early in the evening, but said nothing about the expedition to his father, whom he had not yet forgiven for his intention to marry again.

A week or two passed, and one morning Will was startled by his father's saying to him, "Will, my boy, I fear me I shall anger ye, but I expect to bring her that'll be my wife home after our next trip. The captain's lady (poor thing!) is going to take her with her for the last cruise this season; and, my lad, if, after thinking it over quiet like to yourself, ye find ye can give yer father's wife a smile and a welcome when she comes, ye little know how 'twould gladden old Mike's heart. Good-bye, and God bless ye, Will; ye're very dear to me, but home can't be home without a woman in it; and you'll love her, boy, I know ye will.

Another minute, and Mike was gone and Will sat down to think. His father's parting words had touched him; there was an unusual tenderness in them. Now, for the first time, it occurred to him that Mike had not looked well lately; doubtless he missed the carefully prepared food and the various little comforts of a well-ordered home. And ever mixing and chiming in, as it were, with these thoughts, came the recollection of a chapter in the Book of Jonah (to which he had listened in the village church only the day before), where God, after sparing the great city of Nineveh, and its many inhabitants, asks the prophet, mourning over his withered gourd, "Doest thou well to be angry?"

"I'm a selfish fellow, and no mistake," said Will to himself, severely. "If mother could speak now, she'd tell father to try and be happy, and me to help him; and here I've been goin' on like a fool. I needn't love mother no less because of father's bringing home some one else. 'Doest thou well to be angry?' No, Lord; it was wicked, very wicked, and I'm sorry." And Will dropped down on his knees at the chair, as he had often knelt, in happy years gone by, at his mother's feet, and prayed for forgiveness and strength to do right.

The day came on which Mike was to bring home his bride; and Will, after seeing that the cottage was looking its best and tidiest, went down to the jetty to watch for the ship. The pain and the anger were gone from his heart now, and in his hand, as a welcome to his stepmother and a token of friendly feeling, he held a nosegay of the sweetest flowers. As the vessel neared the harbour, the skipper fired off a gun, and at the sound the seafaring people gathered in little knots. But Will took no heed of *them*; his eyes were fixed upon a figure of a woman on the deck, who was attending to the captain's wife. Could it be? Yes. Surely he was not mistaken! It was *she* — the kind-

WILL AWAITING THE SHIP

hearted creature who had fed and comforted him on that dismal day of his solitary row.

What a happy meeting it was after all! and how gratefully Will's stepmother returned the boy's greeting and hearty, outspoken, "I'm glad it's you!" And how radiant was poor Mike at the unexpected turn that events had taken!

We should like to go on with this story if time and space permitted, and tell you how happily the new marriage turned out; how the gentle influence of this Christian woman whom Mike had brought home helped Will to a further knowledge of better things, and was the greatest comfort and happiness to him.

There is just one lesson which we are quite sure that the boy had learned, and it was this; that the greatest trials God sends us often turn out the greatest blessings after all, if we only receive them rightly. Dear friends, young and old, have we learned Will's lesson, or gained a victory like his over ourselves?

Waiting and Watching

I WAS waiting and
watching for you, Jack,
For the gleam of your
little white sail;
I was anxiously waiting
and watching —
Last night was a terrible
gale.

And when it was hushed
with the dawning,
I took my old place on the shore,
(The place where you courted me, darling,)
And looked for your coming once more.

And as I stood gazing out seaward,
And sighing in vain for your boat,
    I thought of the past till the tears fell,
And a choking pain came in my throat.

    How well I remembered our courtship,
Our wedding, our home on the slope,
    Our precious wee babe that has left us,
The pride of our life and our hope.

Thus waiting and watching for you, Jack,
    Still pondering over the past,
Still longing to see your frail vessel
    Safe anchored in harbour at last,

There came to my mind a sad picture,
    The thought of One slighted by me;
Of him who had whispered full often,
    "My child, I am waiting for thee."

How often, in years that are gone, Jack,
    That voice had been wooing my heart;
How often in stubborn resistance
    I had bidden the watcher depart.

And now, in *my* sorrowful waiting,
   I seemed to be seeing Him stand,
And knock at the door of my conscience
   Once more with that nail-pierced hand;

While ever again came the whisper,
   As soft as the breath from the sea,
"*This day* thou hast watched for thy loved
one —
For years I have waited for thee!"

So then I could bear it no longer,
   My heart was so sore with its guilt;
I cried, "O my Lord, I am coming;
   Thou *canst* make me clean if Thou
wilt."

And then, with a vision grown clearer,
   I gazed far away o'er the blue,
And saw a white sail in the offing —
   Your boat, my own husband — and *you*.

But I know that as long as I live, Jack,
   And even when time is no more,
I shall think of the lesson God taught me,
   While waiting for you on the shore.

Gabrielle, the Poultry Seller

"I GRIEVE to leave thee, my poor child, my Marguerite; how gladly would I stay beside thee and minister to thy wants, and try to cheer thee! But what is to be done? We must live; it is duty for me to go, and I must trust thee in God's hands." And Gabrielle stooped beside her daughter's bedside, and kissed her fondly. "Yes, it is plain duty; so go, dear mother, go," said the girl. "I do not fear being left, now that all is so nicely arranged by my bedside. Go, mother, but bless me first."

"God in heaven bless and keep thee, my treasure!" said Gabrielle, fervently. "It *is* hard for thee to be alone all day, Marguerite. That comes of our being Protestants — the only ones in this place — and the people shun us."

"It does not matter, mother," replied Marguerite, with a patient look in her great dark eyes. "The only thing I long for is some one to teach us a little now and then. It is so short a time since we two belonged to the other faith, and I want to know more about our new religion. Ah, mother, if only we could read!" and she cast a wistful glance towards a Bible that lay on the table a little way from the bed.

Away went Gabrielle to the market at the town. She was a poultry-seller, and supported herself and her invalid daughter by the sale of her chickens, ducks, and geese.

At the market all was bustle and noise. Gabrielle established herself, however, in her usual place, and commenced the business of the day; but her thoughts and heart were with her child at home, and this gave

her face a saddened and preoccupied look
which people could not help noticing.

"What do you ask for your chickens?"
said a pleasant voice, as Gabrielle was
stooping over her basket to find the little
cloth in which she had wrapped her lunch-
eon. She looked up at once, and met the
eyes of a gentleman whom she recognized
as M. Lecteur, a French Protestant minister
from a neighbouring town, where he had a
church.

It had been his habit to make, twice in
the year, a little tour, and hold services in
the smaller towns, where there was no
Protestant church, and where the few
Protestants there settled had no other
means of instruction.

It was during one of these tours that
Gabrielle had heard him preach, and now
as she gazed into his earnest kindly face, a
thought struck her. "If monsieur wants
chickens," she said, "he shall have the best
of mine; but I have a favour to ask, if monsieur will not be offended."

The pleading tones, the anxious, upturned face, the dark, tearful eyes, said
more than Gabrielle's words, and the pas-

tor replied with a gentle sweetness which
none but his Master could have taught him:

"Tell me what you wish, and if it is in my
power, I will gladly do it."

"Monsieur, we are Protestants," said
Gabrielle, "my daughter and I; but we cannot read, and our Bible lies on the table
unused. My poor Marguerite is so ill with
her spine that she is in bed all day long. She
is very patient, dear child, and does not
complain; her only wish is that some one
should come now and then and teach her
more about our new faith, and tell her the
words of the Lord Jesus Christ, and help
her to be a true Christian. I heard her pray-
ing for this last night when I woke up. Could
monsieur come and see her? I have no
money to offer, but if monsieur will accept
this pair of chickens I shall be glad."

"Nay," replied the pastor, cheerfully,
but with moist eyes; "I want the chickens,
and will pay for them. Believe me, my good
woman, I am well recompensed by my
heavenly Master for any work I can do for
Him. See, the market is nearly over; your
poultry is nearly all gone. I will return to
you in half an hour, and accompany you

home, and spend a little time with you and your daughter."

Punctual to his promise, M. Lecteur returned, and he and Gabrielle walked together to the little village where her home was.

Entering Marguerite's room, Gabrielle introduced Pastor Lecteur, and then followed a very precious hour for these two Christians, so anxious to learn the will of God.

Taking the little Bible in his hand, after offering prayer, the good minister read and expounded the truth, while his hearers sat reverently listening and taking in every word.

As he rose to go, he said, "I intend spending three weeks at the town, as I need a rest and the place has been recommended to me. Now in three weeks, Marguerite, a girl like you could, I think, be taught to read. If I came to give you a lesson every day, would you be willing to learn?"

A burst of grateful tears was Marguerite's only answer, but it was enough for the pastor.

From that day, whatever the weather, M. Lectuer repaired to the little cottage

home, and gave the sick girl her lesson; and
Marguerite learned so eagerly and so
quickly, that he had real pleasure in teach-
ing her.

By the time the three weeks were over,
she could read fairly, if not quite without
mistakes, a chapter in her beloved Bible,
and thus the way was opened for her instruction, and that of her mother, in what
they needed most of all.

"And to think," said Gabrielle, as she
bade the pastor an affectionate and most
grateful farewell—"to think that all this
great blessing should have come that day
when it was so hard to do my duty and go to
market, and when I tried to comfort my
heart with trusting my child in God's
hands!"

The good pastor only replied in these
cheering words from Holy Scripture, which
Gabrielle and Marguerite never forgot all
their lives through:

"Delight thyself in the Lord, and He
shall give thee the desires of thine heart."
"Commit thy way unto the Lord; trust also
in Him, and He shall bring it to pass."

Life for Life

T was an awful storm! The most terrible gale that had been known for twelve months at least; and as it beat upon the coast of Normandy, the sea-side villagers, used as they were to witnessing the war of wind and water, trembled and turned pale, and said to each other, "God and our Lady be merciful to the souls at sea, for it will be a terrible night." Nor was the prophecy wrong; the night came on wild and howling, and when the day broke, there was great excitement among the quiet inhabitants of the village, and numbers of people had run down to the beach, for a foreign vessel had been borne by the relentless force of the gale, on to one of the most dangerous rocks of the coast, and now there she lay, a perfect wreck, the sea making a clear sweep over her with every gigantic roller that dashed in.

"Every soul must have perished," said an old man, who, with sad face and white locks that streamed on the wind, stood gazing, shading his eyes with his hand. "Our people tried to reach them with the rocket and line, after three vain launches of the lifeboat; but nothing succeeded. The ship was doomed, and alas, the crew too!"

"Say, what is that?" cried a fine stalwart young man, who was also one of the party gathered on the strand. "There between the shore and the wreck!" and he pointed to a small dark object in the water. "See, up it goes in the crest of a wave,—now it is gone again. Look once more—it is a man, he is swimming, wrestling for his life. Yes, swimming still, but well-nigh exhausted. My friends, I cannot see him drown before my very eyes, when a plunge and a few strong strokes may save him. Here, quick, get a rope to fasten round me, while I pull off coat and boots!"

At this two young men dashed off for a coil of rope which was kept in a beached boat close at hand, while the brave fellow threw aside all his clothes but his shirt and trousers. But when the people pressed round him, with prayers and entreaties not to risk his life, he pushed them impatiently away, saying, "Cease, I beg of you! Give my dear love to my wife, if I die; but whether I am to die or live, she herself would not have her Michel stand by and let a fellow creature drown, without trying to save him."

Then, knotting the rope around his waist, he ran down into the surf, striking boldly out as soon as the water was deep enough, and as he did so, a woman having just descended the cliff, approached and joined the group.

"Where is my husband?" she cried. "I woke up and missed him; where is Michel?"

The wan light of the early dawn shone

on her pale face, making it look still paler, while her long wavy hair was tossed about in wild confusion.

The old sailor took her by the arm, and pointed to the sea, where a dark speck upon the nearer waves was gradually, but very slowly, approaching another, which only appeared at intervals as it rose for an instant on the crest of a wave.

"Michel is gone to rescue a drowning man from the wreck, Ninette," replied he, gently. "You know he is the strongest swimmer among us, and he has a brave heart and stout limbs, and could not bear the last survivor of the unhappy ship to perish in sight of help. Pray, Ninette, that he be restored in safety to thee and us. Pray for him, child, for he breathed no prayer for himself; how should he, when he believes not even that there is a God?"

But Ninette answered not. Her pale, sweet face was rigid, and her blue eyes were fixed upon the small dark object which was just visible among the huge rollers of the storm-beat sea.

In that terrible hour how many thoughts crowded upon the young wife's mind! But bitterest of them all was the recollection that Michel, in the reaction that he had experienced at finding his religion (that of the Romish Church) so false and superficial, had turned infidel, and now believed in nothing.

As she gazed out seaward, the words of Scripture sounded in her ears like the very trump of doom. "Without God and without hope in the world."

Ninette Rabounes was really an English girl, and a stanch Protestant and earnest Christian. In Jersey, where she had lived before her marriage, she was known by the name of Nina Merrill, but the young Frenchman, Michel Rabounes, had won her heart, and she had married him, hoping to win him, in her turn, to her own faith. So far, however, all her efforts had been in vain, and now he was in deadly peril, and she felt that his precious soul was unsaved.

Unheeded by the bystanders, whose attention was rivetted upon the strong swimmer who, but a few minutes since had gone out of their very midst, — Ninette dropped on her knees in a perfect agony of supplication. Words there were none, but the young wife's heart cried unto the Lord in her pain and anxiety; and it seemed as if, in renewed strength and faith, an answer was vouchsafed, for as she rose there was colour once more in her lips and cheeks, and a brave trusting look in her clear eyes.

Suddenly there was a shout: "God and our Lady be praised! He has reached the drowning man! Hurrah! haul in the rope. Nay, not too quickly, or you will draw them under water. So, so, gently—there they come! Oh dear, what waves!"

And now Ninette could see for an instant her husband's face emerging from the dark raging sea. He was cutting the water with one hand, and swimming on his side, supporting the now insensible stranger. The rope (held by the spectators on the beach), which Michel had taken the precaution to fasten about his waist, prevented his being carried away with the back wash of the waves as they receded, and gradually he was drawn nearer and nearer towards the shore, till being within wading distance, half-a-dozen young fellows rushed into the surf and carried him back, exhausted, indeed, but triumphant, his arm still grasping the collar of the stranger, who appeared to be a middle-aged man belonging to the upper or more educated classes, if one could judge by looks and dress.

We pass over the meeting between husband and wife, nor need we describe the well-known means of recovery from drowning which were resorted to in the case of the stranger. Suffice it to say, that as soon as the first greetings were over, and when the first efforts made had resulted in recalling the insensible form to consciousness, Michel and Ninette insisted upon taking him to their own cottage. In Michel's heart, truth to say, had sprung up a deep interest in the man for whose life he had risked so much, and his kind wife, Ninette, was only too glad to receive him into her little home.

The next morning was as bright and sunny as though no storm had raged the night before. Only the beach was strewn with things from the wreck, and among others a box, which the stranger—now quite recovered—recognized as his own, and whence he took a suit of clothing, so as to replace the garments lent him by Michel.

He told his kind entertainers that he was a missionary lately returned from India. He had landed at an English port, and after remaining there some days, had sailed in a small vessel for Cherbourg, where he had some friends whom he wished to see.

It was when close to the French coast, that the vessel had been disabled by the storm, and driven out of her course and on to the rock. The captain and crew had perished, and it was only by Michel's courage and skill, humanly speaking, that the missionary himself had escaped.

It was on the morning following the storm that he told the young couple who he was; and Michel, finding that the stranger, though an Englishman, was a fluent French scholar, asked him a number of questions about his life and work in India, showing an interest which it gladdened Ninette to see.

Later on in the afternoon, when Ninette had brought her knitting down to the beach, the missionary, whom we shall call Mr. Harcourt, took a little

ON THE BEACH

French Bible from his pocket, and said, "I shall probably be leaving you early tomorrow, my friends; have you any objection to my reading to you a chapter from this best of all books?"

Ninette looked up, her smiling face saying "Yes!" Michel said nothing, and Mr. Harcourt read slowly and reverently from the New Testament selections recording some of the wonderful acts and beautiful words of our Lord when on earth. And as he read, Michel drew nearer and nearer, though he kept his face turned away towards the sea.

As Mr. Harcourt finished with a few words of exposition, Michel moved and came forward, his face grave and thoughtful, and the missionary, rising from his seat, approached him and laid one hand on his arm, while with the other he held out the Bible.

"My good friend," said he, "you to whom I owe — by God's blessing — my life, I want you to accept from me this little book, and to promise me to read it. You have youth and strength, magnanimity and courage. God needs such men as you for His work. Read His Word earnestly and reverently, and you will learn to believe in and to love Him. Will you promise me to read the book, Michel? Surely, after saving my life, you will not refuse me?"

Michel looked up. There were tears in Mr. Harcourt's eyes; tears, too, in Ninette's when she raised them entreatingly to her husband's face.

"I promise," he said, and took the book with a murmured word or two of thanks.

The very next day Mr. Harcourt started for Cherbourg, but with a hope of coming to see his friends again ere he returned to India.

Meanwhile Michel kept his promise, and faithfully read his Bible; and though, with his accustomed reticence, he said nothing to his wife, Ninette was sure that a struggle was going on in his mind, and she prayed earnestly that God would show him the truth, and turn his heart to the Saviour.

One night a letter came to him from Mr. Harcourt to say that he proposed visiting the village two days hence, to say farewell to his kind friends, Michel and Ninette Rabounes, to whom he owed so much.

"He is coming then, dear wife," said Michel looking up; "we shall see that good man's face once more — *thank God!*"

Ninette started in joyful surprise. The *"thank God"* was so fervent, so hearty; such words, so spoken, could never have come from the lips of an infidel.

" Yes, dearest," he continued, in answer to Ninette's look; "I am changed indeed. I cannot resist the love of the Saviour. While I read, it was as if He looked upon me as He did upon Peter when he denied Him: looked upon me with love and compassion; and what could I do, Ninette, but go out and weep bitterly that I had denied my Lord, whose love I had not till then understood?"

Then husband and wife knelt down together, and for the first time there was a family altar in that home, as they gave thanks for the mercy God had shown to them both, and for His unspeakable gift.

Sweet indeed was the intercourse between Mr. Harcourt and his humble friends during the short stay he made at the village, and when he bade them farewell, the young man, turning pale with suppressed feeling, said fervently, in response to a few words from the missionary that touched upon the saving of his life: "Nay, sir, if you consider I did you a service, we are more than quits. *It is Life for Life!* If, by the help of Almighty God, I saved you from death — you, through the same help, have saved me from the eternal death of the soul."

Squire Weston's Brother;

OR, RALPH'S TWO VISITS

IT was well enough known in Eltonville that Squire Weston was a man who had risen. Not that he was any the worse for that — for why should not a man rise if he can? It was by his own exertion, too, that George Weston had risen. Fifty years ago he was in a small ironmonger's shop, a poor boy, badly fed, badly clothed, and worse paid. But step by step he had worked his way up, had obtained an education, studying early and late to improve himself and his condition, until he was master of three flourishing factories and owner of a fine estate which he had named Broadlands, from the number of acres it enclosed.

But, with all his cleverness, his ambition, and his industry, Squire Weston was not beloved. For all his sixty years of life, he had no love to show; and had you asked the people who knew him best why he had won no one's affection, they would have replied that a man who is so much ashamed of the family from which he sprang, that he refuses to acknowledge or associate with his own brothers and sister, was hardly a person to be loved. And further, that one whose unforgiving spirit induced him to disinherit his only daughter because she had married a gentleman with only a moderate income — a man who, in his heartless ignorance, had scarcely mourned, even when his own wife died, because to the last she had borne traces of her early want of culture, and he fancied she had been a clog upon his upward progress — such a man was unworthy of affection, and could command none. But the Squire cared little for this; he was self-absorbed, and the opinions of others as to his character did not trouble him, so long as he maintained the kind of importance which his wealth and position gave him. He never read his Bible, never perhaps had heard the words, "Mind not high things, but condescend to men of low estate," or again, "The fear of the Lord is the beginning of wisdom."

In his prosperity, George Weston had waxed hard and hard as the nether millstone; conscious only of his own superiority over those from whose ranks he had risen, he was lost to the fear of God, to the love of his fellows, to the duties of mercy and sympathy, patience and self-denial.

Alas! Squire Weston, of Broadlands, was in a terrible case, though he knew it not.

One evening he was sitting in his dining-room, waiting for his solitary dinner to be served. He was in high good humour, for he had been going over the estate with his steward, and was pleased to see in what a flourishing condition all his possessions were. "There's that speculation, too, which Mr. Sharpeye said was sure to be successful," said the Squire to himself; "and after all, the bulk of my fortune is safer still, for it is in the Bank. Altogether things look very promising;" and George Weston gave a little hard chuckle, which was his way of expressing pleasure.

Just then the grave, decorous butler entered, saying, "If you please, sir, there's a person waiting to see you."

"Who is it?" asked Mr. Weston: "tell him I am about to dine, and can't see any one."

"I did so, sir, but he won't go away."

"Won't go away? That's queer; who *can* it be!"

"Why, George, who should it be but Ralph Weston, your own brother, as parted from you forty years agone," said a loud voice at the door. "Your servant there was so long in comin' back, that I thought I'd try to get to you by myself."

"*You* Ralph! *you* here? You surely haven't come back for good?" exclaimed George, rising from his seat, and surveying his brother from head to foot, but without stretching out his hand, or seeming to remark that Ralph's was open to receive it.

"Of course I'm come to stay," replied Ralph Weston, a pained look stealing over his honest, weather-beaten face. "Though," he continued, "I must say you don't make my welcome to the old country over and above sweet, considerin' how long I've been away from my own flesh and blood."

"I always think it a pity," said the Squire, in carefully pronounced language, which was a contrast to Ralph's dialect: "I always think it a pity for a man to attempt a civilised life in England after so many years of roughing it abroad."

"But I've made my fortune, George, in sheep-farming and cattle-runs, and I've come home to enjoy it, and do good with it."

"Well, and pray what is a fortune worth without education?" sneered the Squire.

Ralph's rugged face flushed; but he said gently, "I know eddication's a rare thing to have, and sorry enough I am as I haven't got it. But, George, there's such a thing as eddication of the *heart*, even in them as hasn't it of the *mind*; and God have taught me out there in the wilds of Australia where I've been from a lad — that His love and service, and tryin' to live to the praise of His name and the good of my fellows, is the best wisdom and the truest happiness."

"Indeed?" sneered the Squire again. "Well, you're welcome to all the wisdom and all the happiness you can get out of it — for me. But now here comes my dinner, so I'll wish you good evening, Ralph."

"It would have seemed more brotherly-like, had he asked me to take a bite with him;" thought Ralph, sadly. " But it can't be helped. God have pity on him, for in truth he's a man what's terrible mistook." Then he said good evening, and left the house, bitterly disappointed at the unkind reception with which he had met.

In consideration for the Squire's feelings, Ralph Weston did not settle down at Eltonville, though some of his former acquaintances lived there, but he bought a plain, roomy, comfortable house some ten miles away, with a good piece of land for farming; and there he and his wife were soon nicely established.

Hearing how George had treated his daughter, Ralph wrote to her, told her of his arrival, and begged his niece to bring her children and stay with him whenever she needed change of air and scene; "And if," added he, "your husband can accompany you, why, so much the better."

So very soon Ralph's hospitable home rang with the voices of little children, and he was gladdened by the sweet face of his niece, Eva Melford, who henceforth became as a daughter to him.

Meanwhile the Squire went on in his old way, hard-hearted as ever, increasing in riches, and only — like the rich man of the parable — taking thought where to bestow his goods. But the lessons which he had refused to learn when they were made easy and pleasant, God was now about to teach Him by far different means; and after years of unfailing prosperity in worldly matters, there followed a string of misfortunes such as we sometimes see befalling the most wealthy men, and those who apparently stood the surest.

"I think, sir," said the head manager of the factories to his superior one day "that as things are getting dearer — provisions and clothes, and rent of houses — and there is a good deal of complaining which is not altogether unreasonable among our people, it might be as well to raise the wages of the hands a little; we are making handsome profits, and can well afford it, and the work will go on all the better for the workers being satisfied."

"*I* cannot see any sufficient reason for raising the wages," replied the Squire. "If one makes changes every time the factory hands grumble, one may be making them all the time. No, Mr. Penton. I shall not authorise this."

"I am sorry, sir," answered the manager. "I believe it would have been for the best this time."

"*I* am the best judge of that," said the Squire, stiffly; "I ask you for your services, not for your opinion."

"Well, sir, if mischief comes of this, at least, I shall be free from blame," responded Mr. Penton, as he took his leave, "for I have done what I could."

And mischief did come of it. The wages, not increased by a single penny, were paid as usual on Saturday evening; and on Monday all the hands had struck, and not a man or woman was at his or her post, and the works were standing.

The Squire heard the news without much emotion.

"I'll starve them back to work, and they'll be glad to return on lower terms still," he thought. "It will be good, and only good, for my pocket in the end."

It is said that misfortunes never come singly, and the cup of George Weston's prosperity, after being filled to overflowing, was about to be emptied almost to its last drop.

The absolute failure of the Bank where the whole of his ready money was deposited, was the next piece of news that came to his ears; and before he had recovered even partially from this blow, he learned that the great speculation in which he, in company with others, had been engaged, had come to nothing, sweeping away, as with an avalanche, many thousands of pounds.

Utterly impoverished with these repeated losses, nothing remained to him but to sell Broadlands, and with the proceeds, united to such fragments of his broken fortune as could be gathered up, to go away and live quietly in some place where he was unknown.

It was now, in these days of bitter trial and loss, that there came to him the

remorseful remembrance of his long selfish
life, of his cold hard-heartedness, of his
narrow, limited alms, of his thanklessness
towards God who had given him all, and
who had seen fit to take it away.

Now, too, this hard heart, which no
amount of success could melt, softened
under the touch of God's afflicting hand,
and for the first time in his life he was
humble and contrite.

Quite broken down, he was sitting in his
library one day, leaning his aching head in
his hands, and wishing that he had not
driven from him in those years gone by all
his nearest kindred, and that he could but
have some one with him of his own flesh
and blood, to comfort and cheer him in this
bitter hour.

He was sitting thus well nigh
heartbroken, almost hopeless, when he
heard a step on the stairs, then a knock at
the door, and then a kind, familiar voice
said, with its old hearty ring, "Why, Brother
George, what's all this? I've just heard the
bad news; such a heavy trial for you, dear
old fellow; but don't be down-hearted. I
met your lawyer as I come into town, and
when he told me Broadlands was to be sold,

I said he were to offer it to no one, for I should buy it myself, and you can live here still and consider it your own, and pay me back a little at a time, as you get the money. And there's another thing as I've took the liberty of doing, George. I called round at Penton's house (he's an old friend of my wife, you know), and told him he'd better set the factories running at once, offering a little advance of wages to the hands. I thought you wouldn't mind if I paid it myself. You can't afford, just now, to lose the profits these factories would bring. And one thing more, George. My dear niece, Eva Weston that was, begged me to ask if she might come and see you, and if there wasn't nothing she couldn't do for you. And she sent you her dear love; and the little ones sent kisses to their 'Danpa'"

But this was too much for the poor Squire. Grasping with both hands the great brown palm held out to him, he could only falter out, "Oh, Ralph! Ralph! This from you! And from Eva, too, whom I have treated so badly! God forgive me!"

"Don't take on so, George, old boy!" said Ralph, laying a hand on his brother's bowed grey head. "The good Lord forgives all who really seek forgiveness, and as for me and Eva, why, I rather think, if we ever had aught to forgive, that it's forgot, too, by this time, for I don't seem to remember nothing whatsomever."

Never had the most refined language sounded so sweetly in the Squire's ears, as Ralph's bad grammar now, spoken in that genial, hearty voice of his, as he poured the words — common and uneducated as ever — but full of sympathy and Christian charity, into the lowly man's ears and heart.

And as Naaman, the Syrian leper, emerged from Jordan's turbid stream renewed and vigorous, his flesh as a child's again, so from the troubled floods of affliction this man, into whose heart the canker of pride and obstinacy was eating its stealthy way — came forth meek and humble, his spirit like that of a child once more.

All that need further be told of Squire Weston's history can be stated in a few words. Ralph bought Broadlands, but George refused to retain it alone. He insisted that Ralph and his wife should come and live there, while he considered himself their guest.

Of the welcome — after so long a separation — between the Squire and his daughter, we need scarely speak. Nor need we describe the kindness with which her worthy husband was met when he too arrived.

The children grew up as fond of "Danpa" as though he had never been hard or unkind to their parents. And as for Ralph, though to his dying day he felt and showed his want of "eddication," as he persisted in calling it — still his brother George was wont to say, in a hearty fashion very unlike his old cold measured words,

"My brother Ralph is a glorious fellow for there is one thing that he does not know how to do, and another that he does; and both are equally to his credit. He does *not* know how to bear malice, and he *does* know — thank God — how to forgive."

To order additional copies of **Honesty the Best Policy**, complete the information below.

Ship to: (please print)

Name _____

Address _____

City, State, Zip _____

_____ copies of **Honesty** @ \$5.95 each \$ _____

Postage and handling @ \$1.35 first book
(\$0.50 for each additional copy to same address) \$ _____

North Carolina residents add 6% tax \$ _____

Total amount enclosed \$ _____

*Make checks payable to **Elizabeth Collins***

The Young Advent Pilgrims' Bookshelf
Elizabeth A. Collins
649 Paw Paw Rd.
Marshall, NC 28753

To order additional copies of **Honesty the Best Policy**, complete the information below.

Ship to: (please print)

Name _____

Address _____

City, State, Zip _____

_____ copies of **Honesty** @ \$5.95 each \$ _____

Postage and handling @ \$1.35 first book
(\$0.50 for each additional copy to same address) \$ _____

North Carolina residents add 6% tax \$ _____

Total amount enclosed \$ _____

*Make checks payable to **Elizabeth Collins***

The Young Advent Pilgrims' Bookshelf
Elizabeth A. Collins
649 Paw Paw Rd.
Marshall, NC 28753